1   Breasting the hill: the journey between Porlock and Ilfracombe, *c.* 1900

2   *Next page* Mr and Mrs Nichols of Edington, *c.* 1890

Victorian and Edwardian

SOMERSET

from old photographs

DAVID BROMWICH &
ROBERT DUNNING

B.T. BATSFORD
LONDON

First published 1977

Copyright David Bromwich and
Robert Dunning 1977

Filmset by Servis Filmsetting Ltd, Manchester
Printed by The Anchor Press, Tiptree, Essex
for the Publishers B.T. Batsford Ltd
4 Fitzhardinge Street, London W1H 0AH

ISBN 0 7134 0405 1

CONTENTS

3   Bath: the Roman Baths before their restoration, 1889

ACKNOWLEDGMENTS

A compilation of this kind is not possible without a great deal of help, and the Authors and Publishers wish to place on record their indebtedness to the following individuals and bodies who readily co-operated by allowing photographs to be copied or supplied prints:

Aberdeen University Library (G.W. Wilson Collection) (10); Lady Adams (21); Batsford Collection (7–10, 12, 14, 39, 46, 127); Mr L.E.J. Brooke (86); Chard Industrial and Provident Society Ltd (41); C. & J. Clark's Shoe Museum, Street (50–52); Clevedon Library (85); Mrs G.L. Clifton (40, 97); Mr A.J.P. Crease (124); Mr G. Davies (19); Frome Society for Local Study (45, 53, 57, 87); Mr C. Hall (61); Mr H. Ham (60); Mr J. Hawkins (83); Mr F. Hawtin (27, 66, 77, 126); Miss D. Hobhouse (93); Mr L.W. Hoskins (42, 113); Police-Sergeant January (25); Mr K. Johnson (102); Mr C. Lee (63); Miss E.G.M. Lock (33); Mrs R.W. Mead (68–9); Mr J. Moffat (71); Mr A. Moon (2, 95, 103, 122); Museum of English Rural Life, Reading (Professor John Read Collection) (112, 114, 117, 119, 133); Mr G. Olive (26); Mrs D.M. Parsons (72); Mr T.H.R. Poole (20); Radstock Library (56); Mr G. Rodway (43, 75); Louis Rothman Collection (5); Mr R. Sellick (62, 111, 123); Somerset Archaeological Society (1, 3, 13, 16, 22, 31–2, 34–8, 44, 48, 54–5, 58, 70, 76, 80, 82, 88, 104–5, 108, 120, 128, 134, 137–9); Somerset Area Health Authority (89); Somerset County Council (24); Somerset County Library (4, 11, 59, 64, 67, 79, 81, 100, 129, 131); Somerset Education Museum and Art Service (27, 66, 77, 126); Somerset Record Office (18, 74, 121); Mr J. Stevens Cox (23, 30, 47); Stoke St Mary Parochial Church Council (99); Mr W. Thomas (28–9, 65, 78, 92); Mr W. Vaux (49, 98, 107, 109, 116, 118); Mrs S. Ward (130); Wessex Cave Club (140–1); Woodspring Central Library (17, 132); Wood-spring Museum (91); Mr A. Wookey (6, 110, 115, 135–6); Yeovil Museum (15, 73, 84, 90, 94)

For help in the compilation of this volume, and especially for assistance in tracing photographs:

Mrs D. Argile; Mr Robin Atthill; Mr D.J.R. Clark; Miss E. Dyer; Mrs A. Hulbert; the Revd. D. Hunt; Mr J.W. Hunt; Mr V. Imry; Mrs V. Stevens; Mr W. Vaux; Mr W.E.W. Webb; Mrs P. Wood. Mr J. Thomason undertook the copying or printing of most of the photographs, many calling for considerable technical skill.

While many of the creators of these photographs have now been forgotten, this collection includes some work of local pioneers whose names should be recorded. The value of the work of amateurs like John Hippisley of Ston Easton (135–6), Daniel Nethercott of Beggearn Huish (62, 111, 123) and Sydney Vaux of Seavington St Mary (49, 98, 107, 109, 116, 118) is sufficiently clear by their popularity, and not far behind are Dr F.J. Allen of Shepton Mallet (13, 36) and Hugh Davies of South Petherton (19). Lord Portman might be prepared to pose only for John and Charles Watkins of Westminster (21), but more humble folk went in their hundreds in the 1860s to John Jones of Somerton (30) whose professional standards were hardly less high. Forty years later the local professionals held the field for portraiture and local events, and works by W.A. Crockett (35) and H. Montague Cooper (20) of Taunton, J. Bailey of Ilminster (105), H.H. Hole of Williton and Minehead (129) or Bert Phillips of Wells (24, 82) are common enough. But for the street scene, the real commercial prospect, F. Frith & Co. (7–9, 14, 18, 74) were unsurpassed.

4 Two new bells for Burnham, 1901

5 Gipsies in a country lane, 1890

INTRODUCTION

The years between the accession of Queen Victoria and the death of her son Edward VII were years of unparalleled progress. In a rural county where most of the population depended on agriculture, however, the period was marked by a depression which put farmers out of business, labourers out of work, and themselves and their families out of doors. Many a man went to a better life in some distant part of the Queen's vast Empire. Many a man, too, forsook the land of his fathers and went to the towns, to find employment in the growing industries which even a pastoral county like Somerset could boast. But the country was still there, and gradually farming recovered with the help of mechanization. The horse survived and his waggon, but there were now machines to drill and mow and harvest. It was a different world, different from 40 years earlier, and infinitely different from the present. Only the work of the photographer, himself at the beginning of his career, can recall it with credibility.

Until the late 1870s the photographer was in practice either confined to his studio or heavily encumbered with processing equipment. Instant views are therefore of necessity much rarer than formal groups. The studio photographer, to be found in the larger towns in the county by the early 1860s, reflected the growing vogue for commemorative family albums and 'views' for tourists. In 1861 Somerset boasted 37 'photographic artists', of whom nearly half were in Bath, evidence enough of the gentility of demand. Among them was Mr Budge who advertised 'Photographic views of Wells Cathedral and neighbourhood, Ebor, Cheddar, and Glastonbury. Stereoscopic slides of ditto, 9s per dozen. Portraits correctly taken by the negative and positive processes.' Twenty years later there were 47 photographers in the county, and among the 15 in Bath was one Friese-Greene. Photography was, it seems, becoming popular, for practitioners were to be found in such smaller places as Minehead and Williton, where Herbert Henry Hole was in business. The total number appearing in commercial directories continued to rise for another two decades.

Roll film and lighter cameras as well as improved plates not only produced better quality results. They were also kinder to subjects who found it difficult to remain still, and stimulated the amateur at least to take his own pictures if not to process them himself. Two advertisements of the late nineteenth century illustrate these advances. F. Steggles of Shepton Mallet offered instantaneous portraits of children and declared that he would undertake 'groups, views, animals etc. . . . by appointment'. W.A. Crockett of Taunton offered himself for 'landscape, architectural, animal and group photography at customers' own residences' and undertook to develop, retouch and print from amateurs' negatives, to give lessons in photography, and to provide free use of his dark room. A little condescending, perhaps, but the amateur was at least recognized.

Without the amateur, indeed, this present collection would be much the poorer. The pioneer efforts at portraiture by Mr Hippisley, remarkable early survivals in themselves, are much less valuable to the social historian than the conscious recording of village life by Daniel Nethercott of Beggearn Huish or Sydney Vaux of Seavington St Mary, both countrymen who saw in the camera a way of preserving the essence of their times in the years before the First World War. Between these two approaches lies 50 years of experiment by amateur and professional, known and unknown, between them capturing the formality, and some of the gaiety if not the movement, of many aspects of country and town life. To the professionals belong those splendid compositions, where family groups found themselves in competition with aspidistra and antimacassar, and a bicyclist poses before a verandah of oil paint on canvas. To them, too, we owe the town and village scenes apt for the postcard view.

Yet even an empty street is a record of buildings long vanished or changed, and the appearance of a camera would soon excite the curiosity of passers by. That is a vanished world. No longer will a tripod and black cloth stop small boys in half-mast

6 Motor Rally at Ston Easton, *c.* 1910

trousers, no longer will aproned girls coyly contort; no longer will tradesmen advertise with such restraint, and Goss china and oil lamps be sold in anything but antique shops. But even then it was vanishing, and without such men as John Read and Cecil Sharp the countryside of that world would have been without speech and song; and without Daniel Nethercott, Sydney Vaux and their fellow photographers that world would be lost beyond recall.

TOWNSCAPES

Pastoral Somerset boasted but one large town at the beginning of Victoria's reign, and it was a town, or rather a city, which belonged not to Somerset alone. Bath's attractions, if only gradually recovering from depression at the end of the nineteenth century, were just becoming visible again in the 'rediscovered' ruins of the Roman city and in the fashionable shops. Weston super Mare grew with greater pace from fishing village to popular resort thanks to the advance of the railways and to the people's inclination towards leisure. For the rest, ancient market towns expanded or not as commerce dictated, serving the needs of the countryside on market days but remaining remarkably unchanged and attractive before the motor car shattered illusions and cleared the streets of people.

7 Country town languor: Wellington town centre, 1907

8 *Right* Milsom Street, Bath, 1903: the upper end of town

9 *Right, below* Southgate Street, Bath, 1903: trams and good stabling at the lower end of town

10   Lunch-hour closing: the
Market Place, Wells, *c.* 1890

11   Town church: gas lamp
and a cartload of peat before St
John's, Glastonbury, 1869

12   Town Street, Shepton
Mallet, 1899; even the postman
pauses

13   Back alley: Shepton Mallet,
c. 1880

14   *Next page* Main
thoroughfare: North Street,
Taunton, 1902; shady sidewalks
for a long hot summer

15 Urban expectancy: High
Street, Yeovil, 1883. The poster
on the Town Hall advertises
Bournemouth Bicycle and
Tricycle Club's sports on Whit
Monday

16 *Right* The Quay,
Bridgwater, *c.* 1912; dated by
Bell and Son's hand cart. Most
of the trade was with Bristol
Channel ports and Ireland

17 *Right, below* Weston super
Mare, 1896; the new sea-front
at Somerset's fastest growing
resort

18 Medieval highway: Cheap
Street, Frome, *c.* 1900

19 Making way for progress:
road mending by the market
place, South Petherton, *c.* 1905

THE ESTABLISHMENT

Local government experienced a revolution in Queen Victoria's reign as county, district and parish councils took the place of the Quarter Sessions, county courts and parish vestries which had between them governed the land for centuries. Not everything was swept away in a moment. The Lord Lieutenant and the sheriff retained their traditional roles, judges and corporations continued as they always had done, and the panoply of state occasions was relished to the full. But at a more local level the village constable gave way to the county constabulary and the village stocks and lock-up were abandoned for the police cell. State intervention demanded a registrar of births and deaths, an organized system of poor relief, of education and of road maintenance. Private and local enterprise still fought fires, taught young gentlemen and saved lives at sea.

20   The sheriff and his officers: R. Neville Grenville with H.R. Poole (under-sheriff) and Fred Brymer (sheriff's chaplain), 28 January 1901. The mourning bands are for Queen Victoria, who died a week earlier

21 The Lord Lieutenant:
Edward Berkeley Portman, 1st
Viscount Portman (1799–1888);
Lord Lieutenant of Somerset,
1839–64

22 The judge's escort: the
Somerset Javelin Men at the
Court House, Wells, c. 1863

23 Dr William Francis of Ilchester, registrar of births and deaths, *c.* 1864

24 The county officers, Wells, 1908: C.H. Bothamley (education secretary), W.C. King (treasurer), W.J. Willcox (surveyor), G.I. Simey (clerk of the peace) and Captain C.G. Alison (chief constable)

25 Sergeant Forward and a constable with the mobile police office, probably at Wincanton Races,
c. 1900

26 Fire engine and crew, Wincanton, *c.* 1880. 'Ur looked quite sprack and vitty when the chaps as farmed the brigade hoppied up on to 'un. Dressed up proper they wur, too, w' girt shiny helmets and cwoats wi' brass buttons to 'em' (*Down Whoame*)

27 Civic pomp: town crier and mace bearers, Wells, *c.* 1900

28   *Left, above* The 'Cheltenham' lifeboat at Burnham, in use between 1866 and 1886

29   *Left, below* Burnham College and its young gentlemen, *c.* 1870

30   *Above* Public Health: John Stone of Ilchester with one of John Wheeler Bourne's patent road scrapers, *c.* 1865

31 Kingsbury Episcopi: the village lock-up makes a useful notice board and a dump for the village blacksmith, 1904

33 *Right* Royal Mail: post office and staff, Langport, 1908

32 'Well, Honor, we must soon be going Homeward side by side.' Mr F. Weatherly, chairman of Long Ashton Union (aged 86) and Honor Coleman, a resident in the Union Workhouse (aged 105), December 1906. Mrs Coleman lived until January 1908

COMMERCE

The ancient market towns and the large villages of the county, largely self-sufficient and catering for an incredibly wide range of demand, were not yet moulded into the uniformity imposed by chain and department store; and not yet choked by the traffic. The family business reigned smug and supreme; industry was still foreign to the country town, commerce not yet commercialism.

34   High Street, Henstridge, thawing, 1891. Post office, a house furnisher and two fidgeting children

35   The new Parade Hotel, North Street, Taunton, 1898. The 'Klondyke' omnibus plied between the railway station, the hotel and the hospital

36 Shepton Mallet market
place and cross, 1882.
Standings for traders under the
market house unused, although
earthenware goods were
displayed on the cobbles as in
medieval times

37 *Right, above* Advertising at
Axbridge, *c.* 1895; 'King John's
Hunting Lodge' occupied by a
hairdresser

38 *Right* The Guildhall,
Milborne Port: Norman
doorway and contemporary
notices, 1896

39 The milkman calls; Bishops
Hull, 1906

40 Winchester Arms Hotel, Taunton, 1905. Mr Babb, the licensee, and his wife, bar lady and friends

41 *Right, above* A local cooperative, Chard, *c.* 1905; provident of everything but staff

42 *Right* Family business, Fore Street, Chard, *c.* 1910; hygiene no problem

43   *Left* Village speciality:
lamps and Goss china at
Winscombe, *c.* 1910

44   *Above* Country counting
house: a bank at Porlock, *c.*1905

45   Open in time for
Christmas: 'Dyke's new toy
bazaar', Catherine Street, Frome,
c. 1914

46   *Next page* Porlock main
street, *c.* 1908. Mr Willis, the
postmaster, was also grocer,
draper and confectioner, agent
for the Post Office Savings Bank
and owner of apartments to let
to summer visitors

CRAFTS AND INDUSTRIES

The crafts and industries of the county were all inferior to agriculture and many were dependent upon it. Coal, iron and stone had been dug from the ground for centuries; silk had long since taken over from woollen cloth in many places. Shoes were the advancing business, and light engineering; but agriculture was still the main employer, and without the carpenter and wheelwright the farmer would be without transport, without tools the labourer would be without food.

47   John Stone and his staff, carpenters and wheelwrights, Ilchester, *c.* 1865

48 Ashman's timber yard, Leigh on Mendip, *c.* 1895. Thomas and Alfred Ashman made handles for the edge-tools manufactured by Fussells in neighbouring Mells

49   Sydney Vaux with a three-horse waggon made by him and his brother William at Seavington St Mary, 1903. The cost was £34 15s, including William's time building the body, 300 hours at 5d an hour. ''Tis a waggon I should never be ashamed to zee my name on! Oaken vrame; elemen zides and rowe-board; ashen hanging-pillar . . . all shaped and put together here-right . . . every piece o't. . . . 'Tis a waggon that'll outlive arn o' we!' (Jacob Priddle in *Cluster o'Vive*)

50 James Miles and his sole-cutting machine, Street, 1862. It was the first machine in Clark's factory to be power driven, stamping out rough sole shapes at the rate of 12 pairs a minute. Bronze medal winner at the Great Exhibition, 1851

51 Clark's shoe factory, Street, 1902: the clicking room, where the uppers were cut by hand. The factory was then employing some 1400 people

52 Fred Huish, builder and contractor, and his men, Street, *c.* 1891

53 Ladies at a silk factory, Frome, *c.* 1905

54 At the Timwood Adit in the Brendon Iron Mines, *c.* 1909

55   Ham Hill, *c.* 1905. The famous golden limestone was quarried here from Roman times until after the Second World War

56   Writhlington Colliery, Radstock, *c.* 1900. The signal box was later re-named Writhlington and Bray's Down

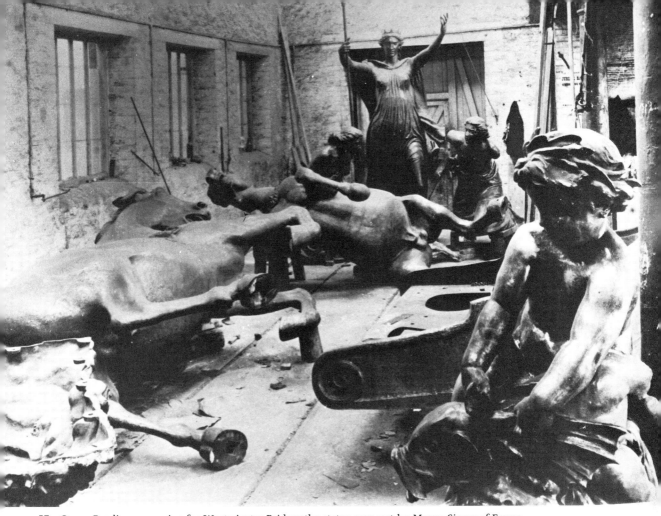

57 Queen Boadicea preparing for Westminster Bridge: the statue was cast by Messrs Singer of Frome,
1902

THE CHURCH

Religion played an important part in the life of the community before the First World War, and churches and chapels were more popular after Victorian revival than they had been for years. Restorations and missions, bazaars and outings had their social as well as religious significance, and the cathedral at Wells and the romantic ruins at Glastonbury were focal points of celebrations of more than local interest.

58 Dowlish Wake church and parishioners, before restoration in 1861–2

59   St Mary Magdalene,
Taunton, c. 1861: the bells were
housed in the wooden cage over
the porch while the tower was
dismantled and rebuilt

60   George Alfred Denison,
archdeacon of Taunton and
vicar of East Brent 1845–96. He
established the first Harvest
Home in 1857, attracting up to a
thousand at a time

63 'The Cathedral', Burnham, and its congregation of fishermen, *c.* 1900

61 *Left, above* The Chew Magna bells in transit, 1898. They were recast by Messrs Mears and Stainbank

62 *Left, below* Mission to the Brendons: Church Army caravan at Roadwater, *c.* 1900

66 The Revd R. Squires, minister of Ebenezer Bible Christian chapel, Taunton and passive resister, returning to Taunton Station from prison, 25 May 1907

64 *Left, above* Congresbury church bazaar, 1904

65 *Left, below* Mission on the beach: the Children's Special Service Mission at Burnham, 1906

67 Glastonbury: the Archbishop of Canterbury (Frederick Temple) and clergy, celebrating the 1300th anniversary of St Augustine's Mission, 1897

69 *Right* Wells Bishopric Millenary, 22 June 1909: the Prince and Princess of Wales at the Market Place, Wells, with the Lord Lieutenant (the Marquess of Bath) and the Bishop of Bath and Wells (G. W. Kennion)

68 Wells Bishopric Millenary, 22 June 1909: Glastonbury Abbey ruins are returned to the ownership of the Church

TRANSPORT

Victorian and Edwardian England witnessed a transport revolution, the effects of which were felt in one way or another by all. The railway, the bicycle and the motor car, with their attendant social and commercial possibilities, shrank distances between village and town and opened the very heart of the countryside. Until well after the First World War the motor car was only for the fortunate few, but railway excursions and bicycle rallies were for more popular tastes. The horse still held its own on the farm and with the carrier; and extreme youth and age demanded traditional locomotion.

70   Springtime of life: perambulating in Victoria Park, Bath, *c.* 1905

71   Mr J Moffat, founder of the Yeovil bicycle firm, on a *Lovelace* machine made at Henstridge,
c. 1895. A studio portrait with painted backdrop and animal casualty

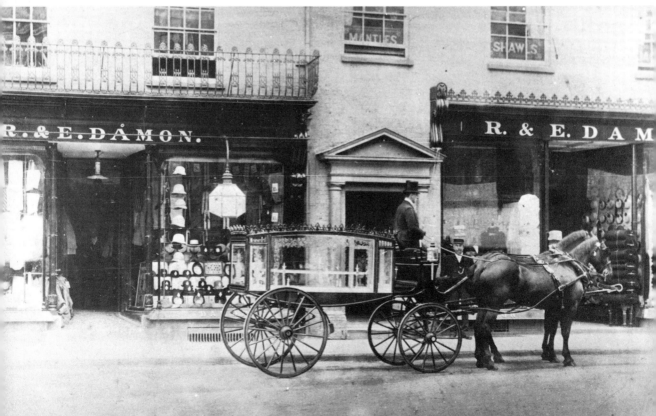

72　*Left, above* Full circle:
William Woolfryes, solicitor,
Banwell, in donkey cart, *c.* 1901

73　*Left, below* The final
journey: Damon's new funeral
carriage, Yeovil, *c.* 1900. Solar
topis in the outfitting
department presumably for
another destination

74　*Above* The Pump Room and
Abbey Churchyard, Bath,
c. 1905; chairs at the ready

75　*Next page* 'Four tons of
coal for the Hall' from Alfred
Weeks of Winscombe, coal and
lime merchant, quarry owner
and general haulier. 'Contractor
for hauling by steam or horse
power . . . brakes, landaus,
wagonettes, Pony Traps or
closed carriages at shortest
notice'

76 *Top* The traditional way: the Lynton and Ilfracombe coach leaving the Ship Inn, Porlock, *c.* 1910. The 'motors for hire' were less reliable than horses for climbing Porlock and Countisbury hills

77 *Above* Watchet harbour, before 1876. A broad-gauge locomotive of the Bristol and Exeter Railway (built 1867); iron ore from the Brendons was shipped from here to South Wales

78 Highbridge wharf, 1903

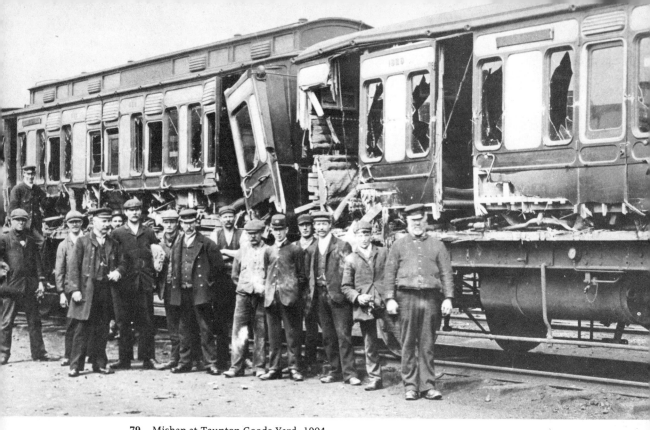

79   Mishap at Taunton Goods Yard, 1904

80   Evercreech Junction on the Somerset and Dorset Joint Railway. This Johnson Bogie Tank was built in 1884–5

81 The Navigators: the Taunton to Ilminster branch of the Bristol and Exeter Railway under construction at Hatch Beauchamp, 1866

82 *Above* Motor rally at Wells
Town Hall, 1901. Cars, a
charabanc and motorised
tricycles before posters of
Edward VII's accession
proclamation and St Cuthbert's
church floral bazaar

83 *Left* The first motor
omnibus in Wedmore, *c.* 1909

84 The Petter family of
Yeovil and their car, powered
by one of the first internal
combustion engines, made 1895.
'There now, if a man had
foretold such a thing when I
was a boy he'd ha' been put
down as a fool' (Farmer Wangle
in *Cluster o' Vive*)

FORMAL OCCASIONS

Formal occasions demanded a photographer; jubilees and proclamations, civic and military events, school groups and family parties all required to be taken, framed and exhibited for posterity often in an unnatural formality which conveys so little of the spirit of the event. Yet they deserved such recording, in an age when every village and town celebrated in style not only the highlights of royal jubilees and a coronation, but also the more common events of a society wedding or the end of term at school.

85 *Below* The Revd F.M. Hargreaves marries Mary Elizabeth, daughter of Mr Charles Hill of Clevedon. The wedding breakfast was at Clevedon Hall, 25 August 1885

86 *Right* Residents of Richard Huish's Almshouses, Taunton, *c.* 1880

87 *Right, below* Selwood School, Frome, *c.* 1890. The headmistress, Mrs Coombs, and her four daughters ran the establishment

88 *Left* The 25th (West Somerset) Company of Imperial Yeomanry ready to embark for South Africa, Taunton, 8 March 1900. Sergeant Howell, standing in front of the company, was awarded the DSO for his part in quelling a native rising in West Africa

89 *Left, below* Richard Axford, surgeon, of King Square, Bridgwater, 1865. He worked at the town's hospital at Salmon Parade

90 Lizzie Little wins the donkey derby: Golden Jubilee celebrations, Newton Road, Yeovil, June 1887. The cart was presented to Lizzie by her friends

91 *Next page* Opening of Knightstone Baths, Weston super Mare, June 1902

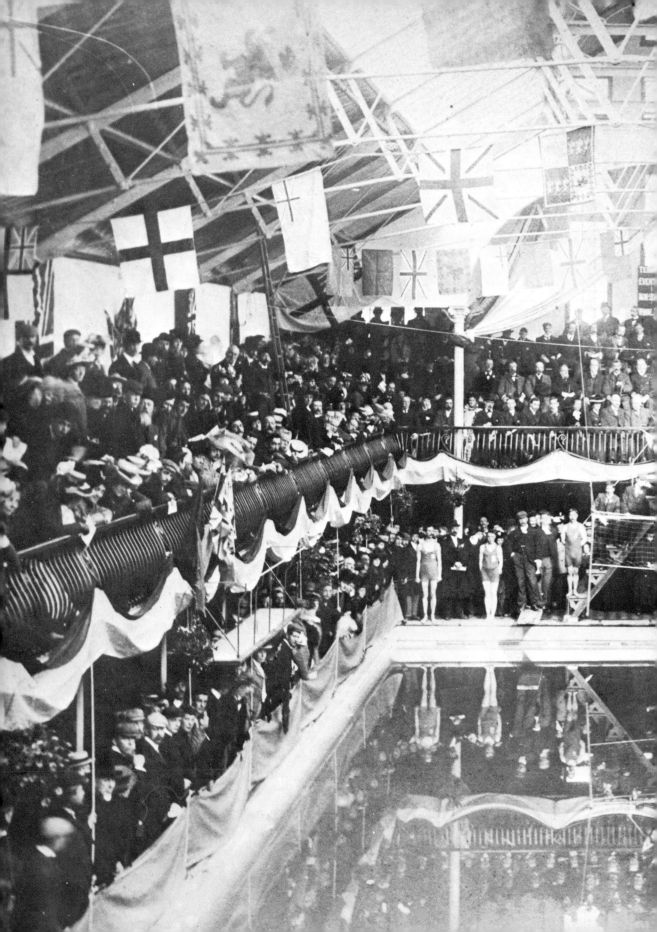

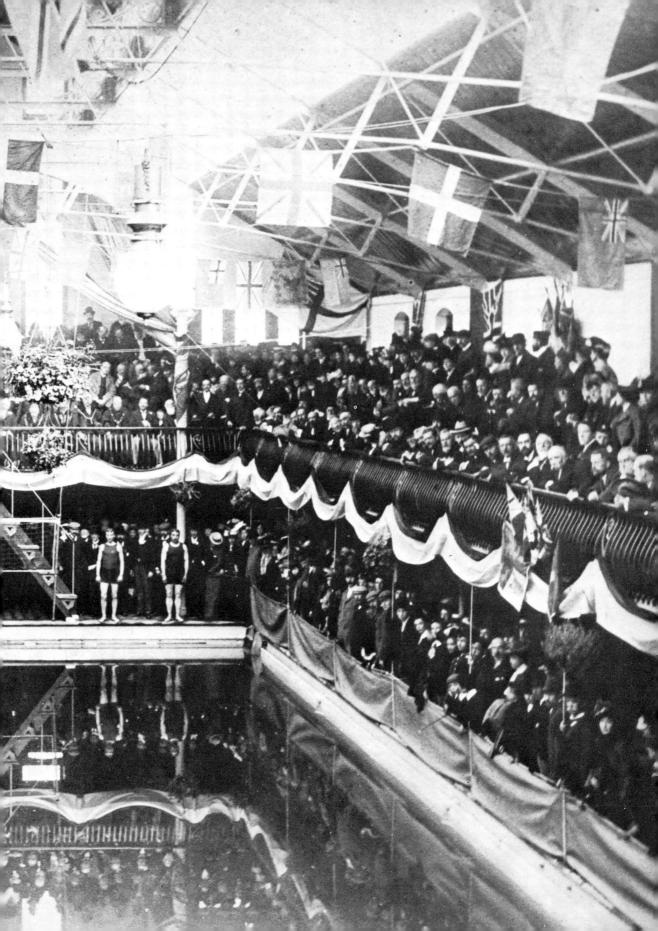

92 *Left, above* Diamond
Jubilee tableau, Burnham, 1897;
Mrs Jarley's Waxworks

93 *Left, below* Pomp and
circumstance: the Bishop of
Bath and Wells opening the
new Recreation Ground, Wells,
22 August 1888. The mayor of
Wells and Archdeacon Denison
are on the platform, cathedral
school boys and civic officials
below

94 King Edward VII
proclaimed at Yeovil: the
Borough, 31 January 1901

THE VILLAGE COMMUNITY

The village was a self-contained community, from landowner to labourer its social structure an epitome of England. To its squire, its parson and its prosperous farmers it owed its school and its almshouse, its charities and much of its entertainment. Its women served in kitchen and parlour or sewed gloves and shirts; its men worked in garden, workshop or farm. The business of the day, the week and the year was the same. Small wonder that Club Day in Somerset villages was such an attraction that schools closed and farming almost came to a standstill. The band played, club members tied favours to brass-headed poles, processions formed calling at one farmhouse and then another, ending up on the squire's lawn for a photograph. Cider and beer were free that day, and the tea in a marquee was on the parson and the club. More than one school teacher recorded a heavy crop of absentees on the following morning.

96   The Big House, interior: the Great Hall at St Audries, West Quantoxhead, home of Captain Sir Alexander Acland Hood, MP JP DL. Victorian Gothic at its height

95   The Big House, exterior: Edington House, *c.* 1870

97 *Left, above* The Big House staff: Watts House, Bishops Lydeard, 1910, home of Lt Col Dennis Fortescue Boles JP

98 *Left, below* Church education: the rector visiting Seavington St Michael school, *c.* 1905

99 A faithful servant: Miss Anne Willey (seated left) celebrates 50 years in the service of Miss Mary Woodforde (in Bath chair), Stoke St Mary, 1902

100 Lady helpers at a Congresbury bazaar, 1904

102   Late summer blooms: the ladies of Hinton St George almshouses in their garden, *c.* 1910

101   *Left* State education: the girls' knitting class, Bradford on Tone Board School, 1898

103   *Left* Break for a sup: loading peat near Ashcott

104   *Above* The Marvel: presiding over the tea urn at Drayton, *c.* 1905

105   Bride and groom, Seavington St Mary, *c.* 1910

106 The head of the procession: Club Day at Henstridge, May 1895. 'Zo off they started, two by two, Wi' painted poles and knots of blue, An' a girt silk vlag' (*Down Whoame*)

107 *Right, above* The procession halts: posing at Manor Farm, Seavington St Mary, 1908. Members with their brass-headed poles and ribbons stand on the wall, band and attendants beside and below. 'A little revel like, an' we warmed up our hearts wi' a drop o't an' had a merry time' (*Wold Ways A-Gwain*)

108 *Right* Consequences: the end of the procession, Club Day at Barrington, 1907. The photographer, commissioned to produce a record of the whole event, wrote: 'He was quite unconscious of been taken, been full of *cider*'

109 *Left, above* The accompaniment of all revelry: West Monkton fife and drum band, *c.* 1912

110 *Left* George Wyatt and his wife, of White Cross, West Harptree. George sang *The Rambling Sailor* for Cecil Sharp, but could only remember two verses

111 Converting the young: Church Missionary Society caravan in the Brendons. The use of an eclipse to point a moral suggests a date of *c.* 1905. There were eclipses in that year and in 1900

ON THE LAND

The last decade or so of the nineteenth century witnessed the steady climb of agriculture out of the depression of the 1870s. Somerset was a pastoral county, its famous cheese and cider the product of a damp and mild climate, good grass and hay, and plentiful orchards. The new machinery which seemed to threaten so many workers was probably less of a danger to them than the cider which formed part of their wages. The 'hurry-push' of progress did not affect all farmers at once, and the introduction of a few machines still left much work to be done by hand, especially at haymaking and harvest time.

112 *Left* Sixth annual meeting of the Farm Workers' trade union, Ham Hill, Whit Monday 1877. Joseph Arch, founder and president, in centre of waggon, standing; George 'one for the plough' Mitchell of Montacute sits on his right. The master of the local school refused Mitchell's request to teach the children the tune of *John Brown* for the occasion

113 *Right* Man for moke: treadmill at Combe St Nicholas, *c.* 1868

114 Pause for cider: mowing with a 'Trapper' machine near Wincanton, *c.* 1900

115 Threshing near Coley,
c. 1910: horse power, steam,
petrol and 'hurry-push'.
'Dreshing ways have altered,
too, since the wold days. When
I wur a boy, dreshing went
along the whole winter droo;
they used the vlail them days,
and beat out the grain 'pon the
dreshing-vloor. But now 'tis
hurry-push' (Farmer Wangle in
Cluster o' Vive)

116 *Right* Haymaking group,
Manor Farm, Seavington St
Mary, c. 1910. 'Eight or nine o'
em did start in a ten or twelve
yeacre ground vust thing of a
marnen an' volly on till 'leben,
then th' did lie down under
hedge till did get cooler zee, an'
car' on agean till th'd a-finish'd
un' (*Glowing Embers*)

117   Little Bo-peep, near Wincanton, 1896

118   Shearing on Manor Farm, Seavington St Mary, *c.* 1910. Mr S.R. Jacobs on right

119 Pause again for cider: Henstridge, *c.* 1900

120 The Green, Priddy, *c.* 1905. The stack of hurdles, thatched to keep out the weather, waits for the next sheep fair

121   Selworthy, the forge, *c.* 1900

122   Peat digging near Ashcott, *c.* 1900; firkins at the ready

123   Sawmills at Roadwater, *c.* 1900

RECREATION

The camera could not yet cope with the action of sporting pastimes, and combatants requiring permanent records had to pose, often in uncharacteristic stance. Somerset was not especially noted for its sportsmen, but the famous ozone of Weston super Mare and other resorts brought health to holiday makers and excursionists from far and near, while revels in the summer and plays in the village hall in winter were a welcome distraction from the ordered regularity of the farming community.

124   Yatton Ladies' cricket club, c. 1906, with their captain Mrs Pethick

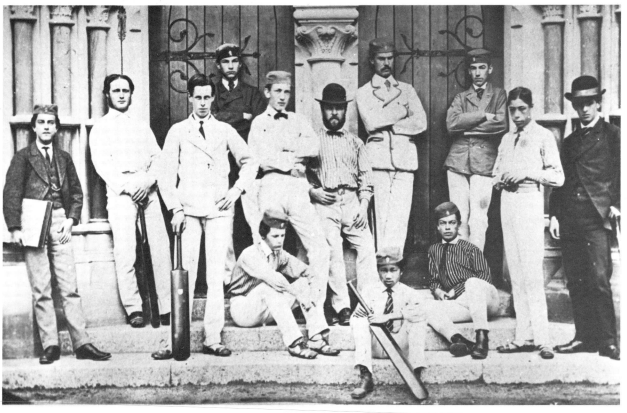

125 Another cricket team at Taunton College School, 1871

126 Photographers at Egford, Frome, *c.* 1905

127 *Previous page* Pigeons in the park: Sunday relaxation in Vivary Park, Taunton, 1906

128 *Left* Pleasures of the people: Westhay Revel, 1909

129 *Left, below* Horse triumphant: the Meet at Dunster, 1907

130 Sport of kings: the winner too fast for the shutter at Burnham, 1892

131 The Slip, Burnham, 1912

132 *Right, above* Weston super Mare sea front after the gales of September 1903: crumpled bathing machines and the Grand Atlantic Hotel

133 *Right* Amateur dramatics: the Camel Players and musicians, Queen Camel, April 1912, in *Conjuror Lintern*, a dialect play by John Read

THE FACE OF THE PEOPLE

Pioneers in many fields: from photography to pottery in 60 years of change. Mr Hippisley's science developed beyond recognition; Mr Gough's cave and Mr Balch's discoveries have an increasing following; Sir Henry Irving a ghost in the gods. Somerset men all, by birth or by adoption, honoured in their generations.

134 *Left* Thomas Clark of Wembdon (1793–1864); a celebrated botanist

135 *Above* Mr John Hippisley, FRS FRAS (1804–98); a self portrait, *c.* 1848. Mr Hippisley, a pioneer photographer, was High Sheriff of the county in 1856 and author of a tract on the Church of England (1851)

136 Anne or Charlotte Hippisley, one of Mr Hippisley's daughters, *c.* 1848

137 *Left* Sir Henry Irving, actor (1838–1905); born John Henry Brodribb at Keinton Mandeville, knighted 1895

138 *Above* Walter Bagehot, economist and journalist (1826–77). Born and died at Langport; deputy recorder of the corporation 1872–7

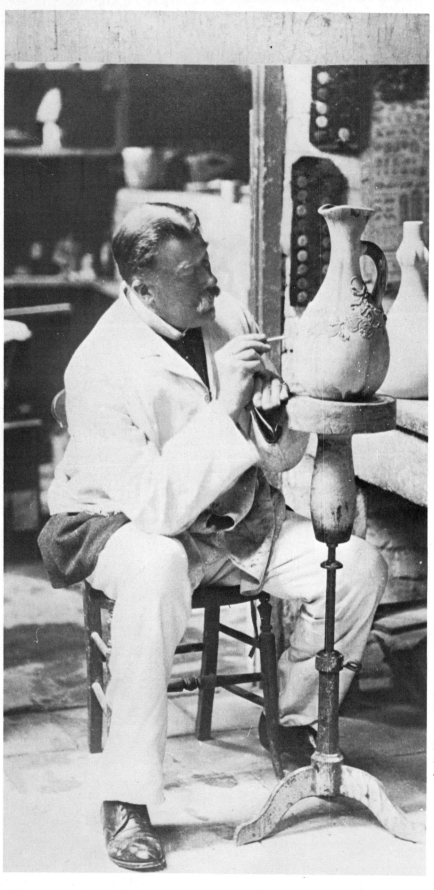

139 Sir Edmund Elton Bt (1846–1920) of Clevedon Court, *c.* 1910; in his studio working on Elton Ware, the only art pottery produced in Somerset

140 *Right* Richard Cox Gough, 1894. Discovered the cave named after him in Cheddar Gorge, 1893

141 *Next page* Herbert Ernest Balch (1869–1958), pioneer of Mendip caving, with his wife and child, *c.* 1900